2.35

P9-CQQ-155

Starting to Paint in Oils

Starting to Paint in Oils
John Raynes

Studio Vista   London
Watson-Guptill Publications   New York

General editor Jean Richardson
© John Raynes ARCA MSIA 1966
Published in London by Studio Vista Limited
Blue Star House, Highgate Hill, London N19
and in New York by Watson-Guptill Publications
165 West 46th Street, New York 10036
Library of Congress Catalog Card Number 66-13004
Set in Folio Grotesque 8 and 9 pt.
Printed in the Netherlands
by N.V. Grafische Industrie Haarlem

Contents

1 Introduction

Painters work in a great variety of ways. They reflect what they see in terms which vary from near-photographic reportage to highly inventive and emotive shapes which retain only very tenuous links with the original visual experience, or perhaps none at all. Some artists ignore the external world altogether, and paint non-figurative or abstract pictures which come entirely from within, without any direct reference to something seen.

It is assumed, however, for the purpose of this book, that you wish to know how to approach the problem of painting objectively, that is, painting with reference to what is seen, and in such a way that the painting does not depart from the original so much as to be unrecognizable.

Changed it will be though: never forget this. Even a severely objective painting *translates* a visual experience, in the sense that a series of marks on a flat surface have to be devised to *represent* the three-dimensional objects which are seen by the artist. Moreover, what is seen varies with the sensibility and tastes of the observer. Our perception of the visual world is extremely selective. We only admit those aspects that we have been taught or have learnt to perceive.

I hope, in this book, as well as being technically informative, to suggest ways of looking at the external world which may perhaps be a little unfamiliar to you as a beginner in painting, but which will most probably eventually become second nature.

2 Equipment and materials

The tools and materials used by painters are as varied and unpredictab'> as their approaches to painting. However there are certain standard, easily obtainable items which have been found to be generally good on most occasions. On the opposite page I have drawn the ferrule end of some of the more usual brushes. They are drawn actual size and represent the minimum range that one should try to get along with. The brushes used for oil painting generally have much longer handles than other brushes, so that one can extend the length of the arm and keep far enough away from the painting to be able to see the whole thing at once.

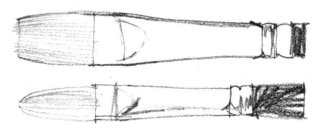

Both these brushes are of hog bristle. The top one is a long flat bristle and the lower one is called a flat filbert. Make sure you clean your brushes after use with turpentine and soap and warm water.

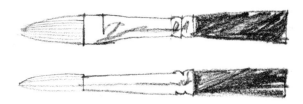

The upper brush is a smaller filbert hog bristle. The one underneath is a round hog bristle. Any hog brushes smaller than these in my opinion are virtually useless.

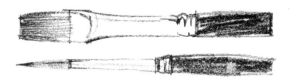

These brushes are made of sable hair and are fine, soft and springy. Paint applied with sable brushes is smooth and sharp edged. The fine round brush is very useful for drawing into the painting.

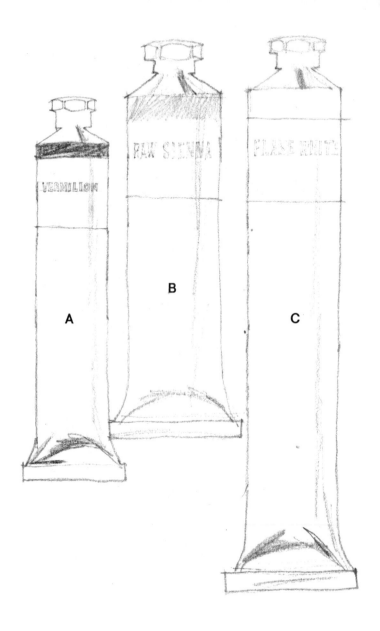

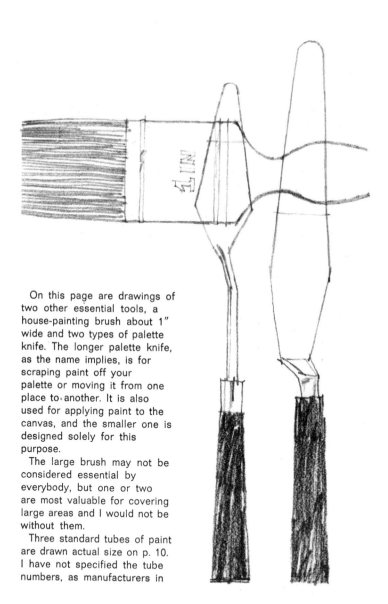

On this page are drawings of two other essential tools, a house-painting brush about 1″ wide and two types of palette knife. The longer palette knife, as the name implies, is for scraping paint off your palette or moving it from one place to another. It is also used for applying paint to the canvas, and the smaller one is designed solely for this purpose.

The large brush may not be considered essential by everybody, but one or two are most valuable for covering large areas and I would not be without them.

Three standard tubes of paint are drawn actual size on p. 10. I have not specified the tube numbers, as manufacturers in different areas may not use the same capacity system, but the tube marked A is about the size of the smallest amount of paint that should be bought, and tube B is better - if you can afford it. Tube C represents the quantity of white paint that most people find to be a useful working unit.

There are occasions when the purchase of smaller amounts of paint than this can be justified, special unusual purples or greens with limited use for instance, but in general it is much better to have big tubes of colour. Little tubes make for meanness with paint, which leads to meagre, finicky painting.

Of course you will need some colours in greater quantity than others, and some are vastly more expensive than others. What you buy will depend on what sort of painting you do, and how rich you are!

The most expensive colours are vermilion, carmine, and all the cadmium reds, yellows and greens, and the cheapest are the earth colours, i.e., yellow ochre, raw and burnt sienna, raw and burnt umber, Indian Red, Venetian Red, etc.

A minimum palette could consist of: -

Flake White	Monastral (or
Cadmium Yellow	Phthalocyanine) Blue
Raw Sienna	Cobalt Violet
Cadmium Orange	Cadmium Red
Viridian	Ivory Black

There are arguments for and against the use of a small range of basic colours. These and other matters concerning the choice of pigments are discussed more fully in the chapter on colour beginning on p. 32.

Turpentine or white spirit, which is the usual solvent for oil paint, will be necessary for cleaning brushes, palette etc., and is also used for thinning paint in the early stages of a painting. When used in this way it is said to be a medium. Another more or less essential medium is linseed oil, which renders paint smoother flowing and slower drying. Other less widely used mediums are poppy oil, which is even slower drying, stand oil, a thicker stickier version of linseed, and copal oil medium which *decreases* the drying time of oil colours. There are also several resin and plastic based mediums available now, which dry very quickly and enable the artist to apply successive layers of paint with minimum delay.

Stretching a canvas

Push joints of stretcher pieces together tightly, making sure that the corners are at right angles.

Starting from the **centre** of one side, stretch the canvas and fasten with a tack into the outside edge of the stretcher. Move to the centre of the opposite stretcher piece and stretch against first tack.

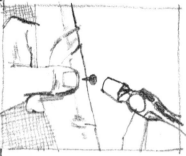

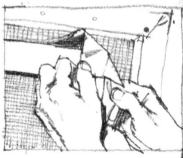

Do the same on the other two sides, then work outwards towards the corners. Try to keep the tension even and the weave of the canvas straight. Fold corners as shown.

The canvas should now be flat with no puckers. Insert wedges in the slots in the corners of the stretcher and tap gently to tension canvas.

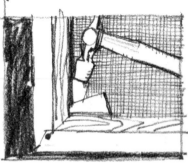

Next, one must have something to mix on. A hand-held palette, rectangular or oval, is traditional. The better ones are weighted and balanced so that the thumb hole is at the centre of gravity, thereby reducing the strain of holding it. Many artists, myself included, prefer to mix on a sheet of glass or plastic on a table top or high stool, which can be much larger and is easier on the thumb! If you decide on a hand-held palette, you must have dippers (cups), which are little clip-on containers for turps and oil. With a table-top palette, a couple of jam jars suffice for this purpose.

Almost any material, suitably primed, will do as a painting surface, but again the traditional material is stretched canvas. Canvas is very pleasant to work on and has the advantage of being able to be removed from its stretcher and rolled, allowing fresh canvas to be prepared on the same stretcher. Its disadvantages are its comparative fragility and the rather high cost if it is bought ready stretched and prepared. It is cheaper if bought by the yard and stretched on a frame made up from standard stretcher pieces, as shown in the figs. opposite.

A pleasant, strong and relatively cheap surface to paint on is hardboard, a building board which is available at most hardware stores. Oil sketching paper I rather dislike, but it *is* cheap.

The priming of a surface preparatory to painting can be a long complicated affair involving several coats of size and carefully applied 'gesso', made up of gypsum, zinc white and glue, but nowadays there are many proprietary primers available, which are simply brushed on. Some of these are resin-based, dry quickly and, being slightly elastic, are therefore resistant to cracking. Many painters prefer them to oil-based grounds.

The best type of easel for indoor use is undoubtedly the 'radial'. The one shown on the far left of p. 16 will firmly hold canvases up to 4 or 5 feet square and is relatively inexpensive to buy. It is too heavy to take out of doors of course, and for this a folding easel is the only answer. No folding easel that I know of is wholly satisfactory on grounds of stability, but probably the easel-sketch box type is slightly more rigid. Remember when buying an easel, that it is most important that the canvas should be held rigid even when paint is being applied to the outer edges. Before

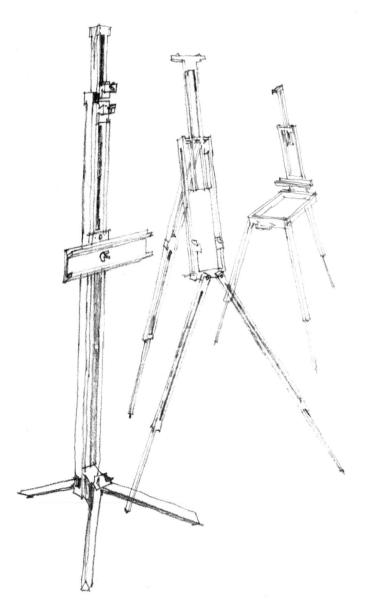

buying, put a canvas or board on the easel and satisfy your-self that it will hold firmly the size of canvas you are likely to work on.

I will discuss outdoor easels further in chapter 9.

Sometimes one can be lucky enough to see for sale an old easel of the traditional studio type (see below). They are large, strong and rather splendid, but rare nowadays.

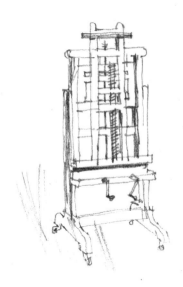

3 Simple perspective

The laws which predict and describe the manner in which objects appear to diminish in size with distance from the observer are called the laws of perspective.

A careful drawing from observed reality, relating shape to shape with absolute accuracy, should in theory produce perspective that is in exact accordance with these laws, even if one is quite unaware of them. But such acute observation without the aid of any rationalisation is very difficult, and the knowledge of a few principles of perspective can be useful as a sort of cross-check for your own observation.

The basis of all perspective is the apparent convergence of all parallel lines at the horizon, and a good practical demonstration of this is a stretch of railway line. The drawing opposite shows rather diagrammatically what you would see if the railway went straight across a plain until it disap-

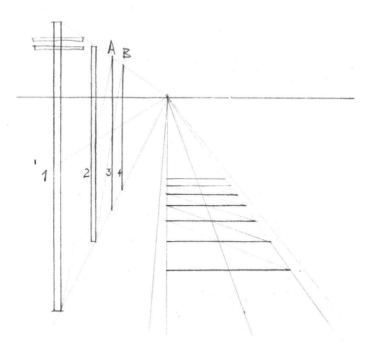

peared from sight. Notice that the tops of the telegraph poles are also in a line which vanishes at the same point on the horizon.

It is assumed that the telegraph poles are all the same height and the same distance from the railway line, so that an imaginary line through them would in fact be parallel to the ground and the railway line. It therefore follows the rule that all parallels appear to converge at the same point. Consequently any line drawn from halfway up any pole or halfway across any sleeper to the vanishing point, will bisect all the other poles and sleepers, and the same applies for any other divisions.

There is another important effect demonstrated by this diagram. The distances between equally spaced objects appear smaller and smaller as they approach the horizon. Suppose that the first and second telegraph poles have

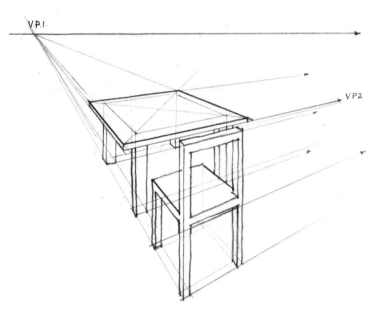

been drawn in, so establishing a pole to pole distance that is to be constant. Then a line from the base of pole one, through a point halfway up pole two, will cut the vanishing line of the top of the poles at point A. A vertical line through this gives pole three. Pole four can be found similarly by a line from the bottom of pole two, through halfway point on pole three to point B, and so on.

We have assumed until now that the parallel lines which are *crossing* your vision will converge to points on the horizon a long way out of the field of vision at *each side,* so that to all intents and purposes they appear to be parallel and are drawn as such. Now, if we observe a straight-sided object such as a house or a table from a position in which the vanishing point of two sides (V.P.1) is to one side of our view, then the *other* two sides will converge towards another point on the horizon (V.P.2), as in the fig. above. If V.P.1 is near the centre of vision, then V.P.2 will be a long way away and the convergence will be slight, but as V.P.1 is pushed further out to one side, V.P.2 comes nearer to the centre. You will see that the diagonals of the table top have been drawn in. Their intersection point shows the true centre, and this is a useful way of finding the central point of any regular four-sided figure in perspective.

21

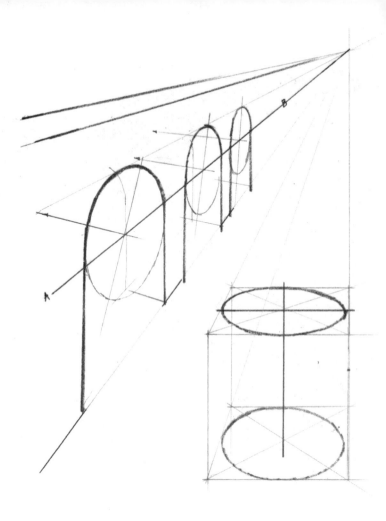

Circles in perspective are called ellipses. They range from very flat to nearly circular shapes, depending on the eye level. Careful observation and drawing of the tops of cans, saucepans, etc. will soon impress on your visual memory their particular character of shape.

The viaduct on the left has been drawn assuming that the arches are semi-circles (true arches never are) so that in perspective they are half ellipses. Notice the position of the ellipses (tipped slightly because their common axle vanishes to the horizon on the left), and the way they are cut by the vanishing line (AB) of the tops of the supporting pillars.

Obviously there is much more to perspective than this. It is a very involved subject, but I suggest that unless you are particularly interested, you should not bother to go into it too deeply.

If, for example, you are looking at a twisting, undulating downhill street, wet from rain, with reflection on the roofs and pavements, it is much easier to draw what you see than to work out the very complicated perspective explanation.

Remember the basic rules, and look very carefully. Then, if you like, forget the laws. Lots of very beautiful pictures have been painted in which the perspective is extremely inaccurate, either because the artist has not known or bothered about it, or because he has distorted it knowingly for his own purposes.

4 Composition

I intend to deal very briefly with composition under its own heading, as it is really inseparable from the whole process of painting and will be returned to constantly in succeeding chapters. Composition is the abstract pattern of the picture, the skeleton which supports the whole structure. Even the most realistic objective painting must have a good basic pattern.

The most usual shape in which to compose is a rectangle, either upright or horizontal. Square paintings are a little more difficult to compose, and other shapes such as circles, ovals, triangles, polygons, etc., while they *are* used, are too unusual to consider here.

The achievement of balance without boring symmetry is the first thing to aim at when composing. Obviously, absolutely symmetrical divisions of shape, such as a square divided into four equal smaller squares, will result in a balanced composition, but unless something very sophisticated is done with colour and tone, it will be rather unexciting and unsatisfactory.

Rather boring division of
rectangle into two equal halves.

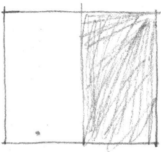

Simple modification to
achieve a more interesting
balance.

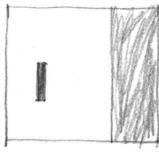

Further diversification focuses
attention on or about the
white square.

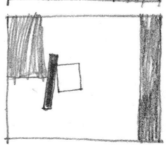

The composition could
continue to evolve into an
immensely complicated pattern,
but it doesn't have to. A
composition may be arrived at
which consists of a very
subtle disposition of a very
few simple shapes.

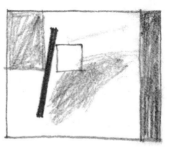

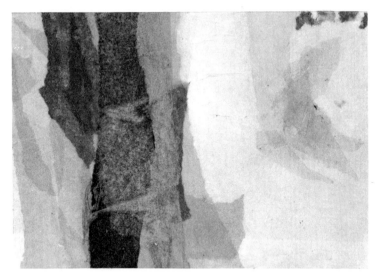

Compositions from torn tissue paper

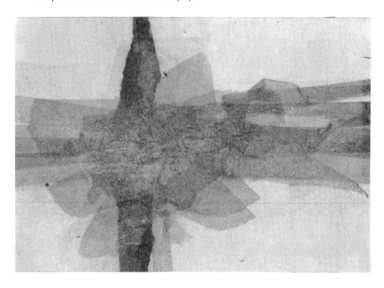

Now, neutral tones and colours and flat or evenly textured areas tend to have less 'weight' in a composition, and quite large areas can be balanced by small areas of strong colours or tones, or of high contrast concentrated pattern. On p. 27 are some very simple demonstrations of the use that can be made of this effect. I suggest that a certain amount of time is spent playing about with shapes and colours in an entirely abstract way, as an amusement and an exercise.

One method of experimenting in this way is by the use of coloured tissue paper, cut or torn and stuck down with varnish or gum. The colours are very clear and translucent, and where one paper is placed on another, the darker colour and tone achieved by the 'overprint' is beautifully clear and clean. The varnish should be brushed under and over the layers of tissue, much as a bill-poster works. Any clear adhesive will do, as long as it can be brushed on fairly liberally, but aircraft dope (airplane glue) is ideal, as it dries quickly and doesn't discolour the paper. Pp. 28 and 29 show examples of composition arrived at by the use of tissue paper. The tones can be diversified even more by adding pieces of opaque coloured paper and multi-coloured

cuttings from magazines, etc. This sort of picture making is known as 'collage'.

Although most pictures are rectangles with the long sides horizontal, many other shapes can be experimented with. The subject does to a certain extent dictate the shape, and in fact the accepted description of the horizontal rectangle is 'landscape shape' and of the vertical rectangle, 'portrait shape'. A standing portrait might need a long, thin, upright rectangle, and certain wide expanse landscapes can be most dramatic on an unusually wide canvas.

Try composing in these less usual shapes: the possibilities are endless.

When considering the composition of an objective painting, remember the lessons learned with abstract shapes. Consider not only the objects and figures, but also the empty areas, the spaces between, which are just as important in the structure of your picture even though they may not be the centre of interest for an observer.

5 Colour

Colour is light. White light from the sun is made up of all visible colours of light, from red, through orange, yellow, green and blue, to violet. Passing white light through a prism will split it up into these component colours, and the range so displayed is called the *spectrum*, all the colours in it being pure 'spectral' colours.

The coloured lights of the spectrum have different wavelengths and frequencies, the hot reds and oranges having the highest frequency and the blue-violet end the lowest. Now, when white light from the sun strikes an object, some of its component colours are absorbed by the material of the object and some are reflected. Those that are reflected are seen by us. Thus a yellow object, for instance, is one that has absorbed all the colours of the spectrum except yellow, which it reflects to the observer's eye.

If all the light is absorbed and none reflected, the object will appear black, and if all the light is reflected and none absorbed, then it will of course appear white.

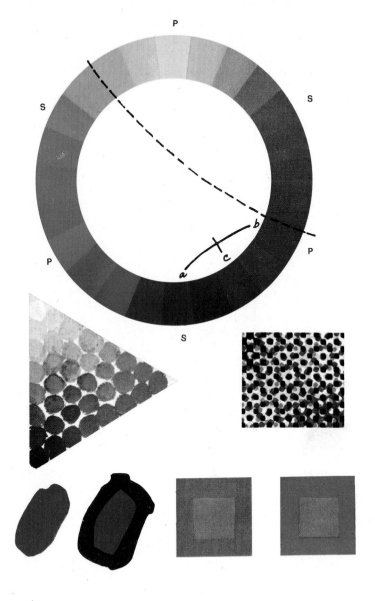

Pigments are substances which absorb most of the spectrum and reflect the remainder, the purest being those that reflect a strong, true spectral hue. These substances, which can be mineral, vegetable or even animal in origin, are mixed with a suitable colourless vehicle and can then be used as paint. If we had a range of paints each of which was a true spectral hue, and mixed them together in the right proportions, the theoretical resultant would be black, because between them all the colours of the spectrum would be absorbed and none reflected to the eye. This is 'subtractive' mixing, as opposed to 'additive' mixing as with light, when all the spectral colours together make white.

In practice it is almost impossible to make absolutely true spectral hues in paint, although nowadays we can approach them very closely.

The top illustration opposite p. 32 shows the spectral colours arranged in a circle, the red and violet being joined by a non-spectral purple (a mixture of red and violet). Three colours are labelled P: these are primaries, and are colours which cannot be arrived at by mixing and from which all other colours can be mixed. They are usually called magenta red, lemon yellow and turquoise blue, and they are evenly placed around the colour circle. Some colour theories postulate more primaries, but the three primary system is more generally accepted.

Secondary colours (marked S on the colour circle) are the result of mixing together adjacent primaries, and you will notice that each secondary colour is opposite to a primary on the circle. Colours which are opposite each other on the colour circle are said to be complementary colours, i.e. purple-blue is the complementary of lemon yellow, and orange is complementary to blue, etc. Complementary pairs are always extremely contrasting and if mixed together will produce a neutral grey.

In order to go further into colour theory, to consider that is, other than spectral colours, it is necessary to introduce some more terms. I propose to use the definitions of the Munsell theory, a very comprehensive affair by American theorist A. H. Munsell, but I will limit my explanation to the simplest basic precepts.

Colour can be said to vary in three ways:

Hue　　　— position in the colour circle

Chroma — strength or paleness of colour
Value — tone value, lightness or darkness
Any visible colour can be obtained by first picking the right hue from the colour circle, then adding enough white to adjust the strength of hue (chroma) and enough black to achieve the desired tone (value).

Most full colour printing in magazines is produced by a process which uses only four colours. The three primaries, magenta, lemon yellow and turquoise, are printed as dots of varying number or size (but equal strength) which mix together to imitate any hue. The amount of white paper showing through governs the chroma, and black, the fourth colour, gives the tones.

The small circle opposite p. 32 is an enlarged photograph of a piece of four-colour printing: this area at normal size would be seen as flesh colour.

I mention this printing method to demonstrate how well the whole colour range may be produced by the use of just three primary colours plus black and white. It also serves to demonstrate another colour principle: the phenomenon of visual mixing. If small spots of two pure colours are placed together, so that they intermingle but do not actually overlap and modify each other, the visual effect from a little distance is as though the two colours had been mixed together before application. A school of painting which began in France in the late nineteenth century experimented widely with paintings which consisted entirely of such separate dots of colour. The system was called 'pointillism' and achieved remarkably vibrant and light-soaked effects in this way. The discoveries have had far reaching influence. Most artists now, while not using the principle exclusively, make some use of colour which is mixed by the eye and not on the palette.

However, to return to palette mixing, it is not usual or, I think, advisable for painters to mix all colours by the printer's method of adding black and/or white to the spectral colours. Instead of using white pigment to weaken a hue, one can use more medium with the colour and paint thinly, allowing the white ground to shine through, thereby achieving greater luminosity. Rather than modifying tone with black paint, use can be made of the natural tonal order. At their strongest, yellows, yellow-oranges, yellow-greens etc., are lighter in tone than reds, blues and purples, so a strong brown can be produced by mixing a little yellow and blue (to make a green) and then adding red. The resultant colour is dark, non spectral and did not require black pigment. A very dark brown will result if a green such as viridian is mixed with, say, carmine. Each of these colours has more black content than a pure hue, and so by using them one *is* using black even though there may be none squeezed out on the palette. All the very dark browns, purples and greys contain black, and to mix them one must use one of the many colours which have a black content.

For these reasons, many artists maintain that black is an unnecessary pigment. I think, however, that it is a very worthwhile pigment if used with discrimination. The triangle facing p. 32 shows the range of tints (hue plus white) and shades (hue plus black) obtainable from a single hue. Another very valuable use for black is as a frame to accent a rich colour. It is quite remarkable how much more luminous some colours can appear when surrounded by black.

So if we assume that ivory black and a white, perhaps titanium white, are the first two essential paints for your palette range, what should you choose to complete it? Obviously the range should be large enough to allow as complete a cover of all the visible colour as possible, and yet not so large as to be cumbersome.

On the next two pages I have drawn a suggested palette layout with the tube colours squeezed out on the upper edge of the palette and the areas of mixing that might result when painting. It is as well not to mix all over the palette in an indiscriminate way. If you do, colours inevitably become muddy and out of control. You will notice that I have placed white in the centre and ranged the yellows, oranges and reds to one side and the greens, blues, violet and black to the other. This separates the palette into two areas, the blue side being 'cool' and the red side 'warm'. The dotted line drawn through the colour circle facing p. 32 divides the cool colours from the warm ones. It is important to appreciate this temperature quality of a colour for two reasons. Firstly, it helps one to analyse what components go to make up the colour to be mixed. Secondly, the conscious placing in a painting of a small amount of cool colour in an otherwise warm colour scheme, or vice versa, is another device in the artist's repetoire of excitement.

I have chosen the range of colours shown on the palette diagram after a good deal of thought and discussion with other artists. Everybody has their own ideas on the subject and they differ widely. However, there seems to be general agreement that the traditionally recommended preponderance of earth colours, excellent though they are chemically, has tended to lead to limited, dull colour. For this reason I have left out yellow ochre, Venetian red and burnt umber, which are normally recommended, and included cadmium orange and cobalt violet, which are not. Bright, clear oranges and violets are very difficult or impossible to mix with currently available oil-bound pigments. This is not to question the beauty of the earth colours mentioned, but I consider they are not as useful for mixing the entire range of colour as the spectral or near spectral hues. An enlargement of the palette could include cadmium lemon, yellow ochre, transparent gold ochre (instead of raw sienna perhaps), burnt sienna, Venetian red, cerulean or cobalt blue, ultramarine, raw umber, burnt umber, carmine or alizarin crimson. This would be a very comprehensive range, but may be found to be too unwieldy. Often an artist will find it convenient to extend his colour range only in the limited band of colour which dominates the picture or series of pictures that he is painting at the time, so that his palette may consist, for instance, of a long series of intense and

Monastral Blue

Viridian

White

Cobalt Violet

Blue Greens

Black

Violets & Shades

Cool Reds

36

Cadmium
Yellow

Raw
Sienna

Cadmium
Orange

Cadmium
Red

Warm Yellows
and Oranges

Warm Reds

pretty blues and greens supported by a minimum of yellows and reds.

I do not propose to bother you with the chemical consistency, compatibility and permanence of paints. Most artists' pigments on the market today can be used together freely, and are also marked with symbols indicating their degree of permanence to direct or reflected sunlight. If a picture is painted on a well prepared ground in thin layers of paint initially, allowing each layer to dry thoroughly before the next is applied, it is unlikely that any disastrous chemical action will occur. If you are particularly concerned about your pictures surviving for posterity, most colour manufacturers publish chemical details of their paints and there are many specialist books on the subject.

Whatever colours you decide to use, do arrange them on the palette in an orderly manner. The order that I have suggested is not the only one, ranging the colours tonally from light to dark is another way, but I think the colour circle order with white either in the middle or separate has certain advantages. These advantages have to do with the clean mixing of colours, and to make this clear I will first describe a useful way to determine approximately what happens when any two pure colours are mixed together.

Look at the colour circle facing p. 32 again. Any two colours which are fairly close to each other in the circle will, if mixed together, make the colour which is midway between them, i.e., purple-blue (a) and magenta (b) will make a purple (c).

The nearer together on the circle the two colours are, the cleaner will be the mixture, but two colours which are further apart will make a greyer version of the colour halfway between. The further apart the colours are on the circle, the greyer will be the resultant, until the exactly opposite colours (complementaries) are mixed, when a neutral grey should result. Remember that this is only a general guide, and in practice, as many pigments are not pure in that they contain some black, the mixtures obtained are browner or blacker than would be predicted by the colour circle system. Not that these 'tainted' mixtures are ugly or undesirable - on the contrary, they can be extremely rich and exciting, but I feel one should mix browns and greys intentionally, not as a muddy attempt at a bright colour. The palette arrangement on pp. 36-7 is virtually spectral, so that the colours which can be expected to produce clean brilliant mixtures are adjacent, and the shades (hue plus black) and tints (hue plus white) are separate from each other, allowing the minimum chance of adulteration. It really is essential to keep some sort of order on the palette, not only in the laying out of colour, but in the subsequent mixing, otherwise the probable result will be a muddy palette and a muddy painting. Of course this might be what one wants, but if so, why put out all those pretty colours in the first place?

Finally, there are a few general principles regarding the use of colour in order to achieve balanced, happy colour schemes.

Hue Use as few as possible. A single hue properly used is very effective. If two or more are used, choose either closely neighbouring hues or opposite hues.

Value Use high value with low value. A variety of values is essential to good colour.

Chroma Use strong chroma with weak chroma. A variety of intensity is exciting.

These principles are part of the Munsell colour harmony theory, and I put them forward tentatively and with the urgent reminder that they are only very simplified principles. I repeat that these should only be used as a rough guide if you are at a loss and have no positive colour ideas of your own. They take no account of the emotional aspects of colour, or colour arrangements which are designed with the intention of being discordant and disturbing. Use the colours that you like, and paint things the colour that you think they are or that you feel you would like them to be, and all will probably be well.

40

6 Light and shade

I began the chapter on colour with the statement 'colour is light'. Saying it another way, light is colour.

Theoretically shade is absence of colour, although in reality it is almost impossible to find completely colourless shade. On the moon, perhaps, where there is no atmosphere, we might expect to find black shadows, but on earth, even in the clearest air, there is a great deal of reflection and refraction ensuring that nearly all shadows contain some light and therefore colour. The problem for a painter is to decide *what* colour a shadow is, and also what colour the light is that is casting the shadow. One may be tempted to paint the light side whitish and the dark side blackish,

Tone drawing of African wood carving

but this is unlikely either to render light and shade convincingly or to be beautiful.

In fact the light side of an object is the true colour of the object and should be painted positively and strongly in that colour. Even when the colour is quite dark, it will still look like the light side if it is painted with clean and positive colour. The shadow side, naturally, is darker, but not always very much so. Frequently the difference between light and shadow is more a matter of opacity and transparency, or warmth and coolness, than extreme tonal contrast.

Here is an example. In front of me are some apples and oranges on a table in bright sunlight. The fruits are close to a pale blue bowl, and one orange is peeled and in segments. The faces of the oranges towards the sunlight are a strong, warm, yellow-orange colour. The shadow sides are not very much darker in tone, but are very much cooler and greener. This cool, bluish-green shadow is largely due to reflected light from the table top and the pale blue bowl. Where the main light and shade areas meet, there is a darker, almost neutral orange-green, and where a green apple is just touching an orange, there is a small shadow which is quite a strong, warm orange-green. The segments of orange are translucent, and their shaded sides which are cool, clear yellow and icy blue look, if anything, even brighter than the sunlit sides. All the fruits are casting shadows on the light table-top, sharp, well defined, pearly-blue shadows, a little darker in tone than the shaded sides of the fruit, but not in the least black. The whole group has a brilliant, bathed-in-light quality. To imitate this brilliance with paint, use strong, warm, opaque, light-reflecting colours for the light, and only slightly darker, cool, transparent, thin paint for the shadow. This is a generally accepted rule for painting light and shade. It may not be the only way, but it is a good rule to start with.

A slight darkening of the tone of a shadow where it meets the light is almost invariably apparent. To show the solid forms of a three-dimensional object, the line of demarcation between light and shade is very important - more important, in some cases, than the actual outline of the object. If the changes of form as shown by the wandering line between light and shade are accurately defined, the edges can to a great extent look after themselves. The drawing of a hand on p. 40 will show what I mean.

What I want you to look for specially, in addition to the colour and tone of shadows, is pattern: the pattern made by the shapes of shadows and shaded areas. On this page and opposite are two compositions in which the pattern of light and shade is the main interest. In the street scene, the buildings and their shadows at the left can be seen as one composite shape. Similarly, all the directly lit areas of the house on the right are rendered as one light tone, thereby isolating the cast shadows of the balconies and the eaves. In short, the contrast has been increased so as to make the most of the pattern. The harbour wall sketch composition is another attempt to simplify and formalize in this way. Seurat, Bonnard, Degas and Matisse (early) are all painters who explored the possibilities of the pattern of shadow in light.

When the light areas are isolated by surrounding shade, one can think of the pattern as being reversed, i.e., a pattern of light in shade. The figure drawing on p. 48 is an example. Here, what I aimed at was a precise simplification of the islands of light within the dark masses, to suggest the form as strongly as possible. 'Chiaroscuro', which means literally light and shade, is a term that has come to be applied to the painting of objects in this sort of light, the greatest exponent, I suppose, being the Dutch painter Rembrandt. When painting 'chiaroscuro', it is very important to distinguish accurately the intensity of the light areas. The tendency is for the eye to see too much and to give all lights equal value. Very frequently an area is mistakenly interpreted as being part of the pattern of strong light because

it is seen to be lighter than the associated deep gloom. When the whole is viewed with half-closed eyes, this 'light' area is seen to bear no comparison with the intensity of the true lights and to sink into the mass of shadow.

Half closing the eyes, thus reducing the amount of light entering the eye, is a very good method of ascertaining relative tones, especially in strongly lit subjects. Always try to look at the thing as a whole when deciding on the value of a particular light or dark area.

7 Painting indoors

Nearly every painting is at least partially produced indoors, so this heading may seem somewhat all-embracing. I mean it only to include the painting of things brought to the studio and arranged as 'still life', and painting based on an interior arrangement as found.

An arranged still life group is the usual subject prescribed for beginners - probably because it stays still and the lighting can be controlled. Unfortunately, arranging a group of objects so that they make a pleasant and exciting pattern, and yet do not look too arranged and stilted, is not as easy as it looks. I think that initially you should look around and

make some drawings of random groups of objects. Such things as, for example, the breakfast table after breakfast, cooking utensils, vegetables etc. on the kitchen table, children's toys on the floor, your desk before you tidy it up, a heap of oddments thrown out for the dustman, clothes hanging up on a door, magazines, ashtray, cigarettes etc. on a coffee table - the list is really endless. You will find that some of the most exciting arrangements just happen, and that careful placing and positioning is not always so successful. You will also discover, I hope, that no particular class of objects is specially suitable for still life. The terms 'still life' and 'nature morte' imply organic, once growing things, and I personally prefer the shapes of natural rather than man-made objects; but artists have painted everything from ox carcasses to corn-flake packets and found them, or made them, exciting and beautiful.

It is usual to group together objects which have some sort of general affinity. A group of kitchen utensils, for instance, would be unlikely to include a sewing machine, and the rocks, shells and driftwood on p. 51 would look strange with an adjustable spanner (wrench) or an egg whisk. Even such strange, out of context juxtapositioning of otherwise normal objects, however, has been used by artists when they wanted to shock the observer.

On p. 52 is the first stage of the still life reproduced in full colour facing p. 49.

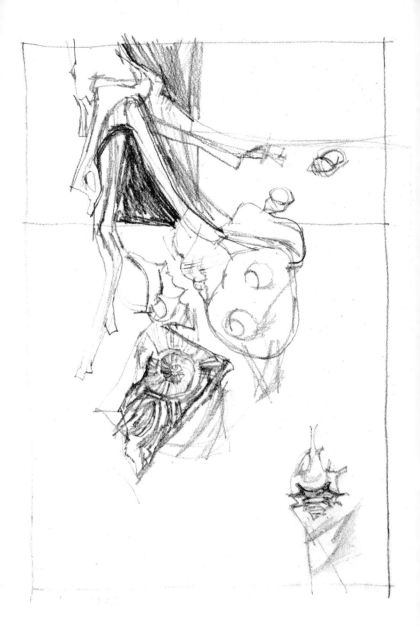

51

In this case I had decided beforehand the sort of still life I wanted to paint, in that I wanted something that would allow me to use sweet, 'pretty' colours - pinks, oranges, mauves, turquoise etc. Temperamentally I am more attracted to dark, sombre colours, and this was a conscious attempt to use colours which, for me, are more difficult.

Accordingly yellow and purple flowers were stuffed unceremoniously into a jug and some oranges, plums, a lemon and some apples in paper were more or less haphazardly strewn around. This 'group' was then viewed from various directions and heights, and its components moved about until the pattern of shapes began to look satisfactory. It is impossible to give much guidance in this matter of 'satisfactory' shapes. There is some degree of general agreement among people of similar experience in painting, but it is a very personal thing and there is also plenty of dissension. All I can do is refer you back to the chapter on composition, and suggest that you use a paper mask when viewing the group to help you decide on the best arrangement.

When I had decided on which portion of the group to use for the composition (see above), the pattern was established freely and abstractly on the canvas (opposite).

At this stage, it is better to use thin, turpsy paint which will dry quickly and can then be overpainted. You must also be alert to the possibility of any of this early, thin stage working successfully without further modification. Such thinly painted areas, especially in the darker passages, are very valuable and exciting as a contrast to the heavier, opaque paint which may be used later. Colour applied opaquely, or over a dark ground, never has quite the same inner glow that enlivens semi-transparent paint directly over a white ground. Sometimes, if such an effect is required later on in a painting, it is necessary to re-apply a white or light area, wait for it to dry, and then paint the transparent colour over it. The application of one or more layers of transparent colour in this way, so that the underlying paint glows through, is called glazing. Colour to be used as a glaze can be made more transparent, if need be, by thinning with painting medium, retouching varnish or a mixture of turps and varnish.

This 'thin to fat' painting method, however, does not constitute an unbreakable law. All 'alla prima' painting depends on the first direct application of more or less thick paint which is then left unmodified, and some painters cover the whole painting area with paint as much as one or two inches thick. It is easier to keep a painting under control if the thick, slow drying paint is worked up to by stages, and it is all too easy for a thickly painted beginning to become a sticky, uncontrollable mess.

In stage 2 of the flower and fruit group (opposite), the main areas of colour have been more firmly delineated and an attempt has been made to suggest space and volume. From now on, to speak of 'stages' in the painting is a little arbitrary, as it is a continuous process of organising shapes and colours, sometimes diversifying, sometimes simplifying, until the whole thing hangs together coherently and is complete. The length of any one session of painting tends to be dictated by the time it takes to cover the painting area. Once all the areas which are being worked on are wet, then it is necessary to wait until the paint dries. An alternative procedure is to scrape or wipe down an unsatisfactory passage, and work on the surface so revealed. Areas which have been painted rather more thickly than intended, but are otherwise satisfactory, can be modified without damage by carefully placing a sheet of newspaper flat on the canvas and lifting off the surplus paint.

black background

cerulean

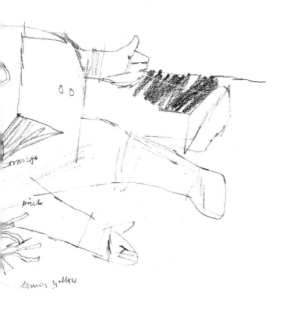

orange

pink

lemon yellow

Random group: fallen high-chair and toys

It is not a bad idea, at some stage, to turn your back on the still life group and consider the painting itself as a pattern of colour and shape independent of the reality which inspired it. Paint what you 'feel' about the still life, and eradicate any details which deflect attention from what you feel.

Be sparing, as ever, about highlighting: even if an eye-deceiving illusion of obective reality is your intention, bright highlights occur infrequently and must be subtly placed. To decide on the intensity of any light, compare it with the whole of the group, not just with its immediate vicinity.

Above all, do not be afraid to re-paint - this is not failure, it is the natural progress of painting.

8 Portrait painting

There is one common mistake almost invariably made by beginners when painting a portrait. This is their failure to appreciate the importance of structure in drawing the head and face. The temptation is immediately to begin defining the shape of eyes, nose and mouth in the hope of achieving an instant likeness to the sitter. In fact, 'likeness' is very unlikely to result in this way. We recognize people by the pattern of all their physical features. Such things as the relative positions of the brow ridge and cheek bone, the length of the cheek from the eye to the corner of the mouth, the direction of the jaw etc., are the most important aspects to establish. In recognizing a face, the actual shape of each individual feature is much less important than you may think.

59

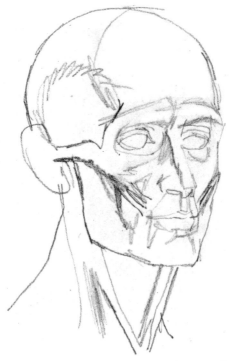

Background heads in newspaper photographs prove my point. Such heads are sometimes composed of a few coarsely modified dots, the shape of individual features cannot be deciphered and yet the face is instantly recognizable. What we recognize, I repeat, is the overall pattern of shape which is characteristic of that particular face and head.

To discover this basic pattern, one needs to understand something of the underlying structure of the head and face. On the opposite page are drawings of the human skull, and on this page is a drawing showing the main muscle forms. I find that a particularly valuable edge of form to detect and establish early when proportioning a head, is that shown by the pen line on the drawing on p. 58. This traces the edge of the zygomatic arch, down the zygomatic muscle and round and under the lower lip. The delineation of this edge helps to find the plane of the front of the face

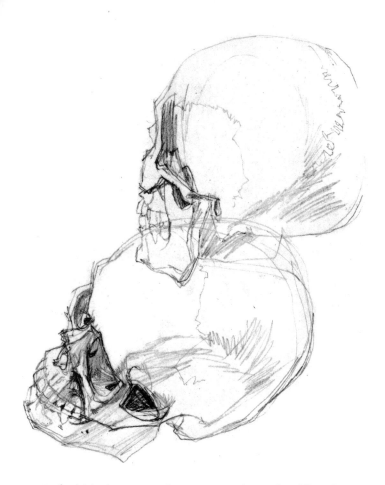

out of which the nose ridge juts at right angles. The plane of the forehead is more or less parallel with the front plane of the face, but stepped forward so as to form a brow ridge.

Remember that the eyes are complete orbs set into bony sockets so that about half or less protrudes. The eyelids covering this hemisphere are form-hugging and even when open, their shape is very revealing and important. The edge of the upper lid especially is a useful shape to draw when trying to establish the position of the eyes. The whole process of drawing objectively, especially the human head, is a matter of careful searching for the exact relationship of one part to another, checking and cross-checking continually until the whole thing sits together convincingly. When painting, of course, this applies to the whole painting area, so that the spaces behind and around the head must be considered carefully at the same time as the head is being constructed.

Portraiture has unfortunately suffered in recent years from the need by patrons for something very close to a coloured photograph and from the willingness of fashionable portrait-painters to give it to them. At all costs do not try to emulate such paintings. I don't intend to argue for painting or photography as the more suitable medium for portaiture, but I think it should be clearly recognized that they are different, they perform different functions, and should not try to imitate each other.

It is not enough for a portrait to be a speaking likeness, of interest only if the sitter is known and recognized. The painting must be interesting in terms of colour, shape, texture and composition: interesting, in fact, as a painting.

On this page are a few of the many possible compositions. Opposite is a simplified diagram of a painting by Degas. It is a portrait of Hortense Valpinçon as a child, and is a good example of the type of composition in which the head itself is just one of a group of surrounding objects and shapes of equal compositional

importance. In such a composition the human head will nearly always hold its own in interest, even when the surrounding objects are large and numerous.

The tall composition is from a picture painted in 1919 by Amedeo Modigliani called *Boy with Red Hair*. It exemplifies his practice of elongating and simplifying figures while retaining their essential character.

The third composition is that of a portrait by Jan van Eyck, a fifteenth-century Flemish painter. His use of the triangular shape of head and head-dress is obvious and compelling.

Stage 1

The first exploratory lines and tones are made with very thin 'turpsy' paint. In this way the whole composition can be moved about to find the best disposition of the big shapes.

Stage 2

Now some slightly thicker paint can be used, but very little if any white paint is used at this stage, in order to keep all the colours transparent and clear.

Stage 3

Colours mixed with white and therefore opaque are now gradually introduced where necessary to strengthen the form. In general it is better to keep the paint in the shadow areas thin and transparent, making use of the first underpainting wherever possible.

Stage 4

9 Painting outdoors

Before going into the country or town to paint a subject on the spot, it is essential to get organized. A certain amount of disorganization or even confusion can be tolerated in your painting room, but when miles from base or the nearest hardware shop, it is most infuriating to find that the turps or some other essential has been left behind. The only way to ensure that this does not happen is to be scrupulously methodical.

Ideally, the complete outdoor painting kit should be separate from the studio equipment and always packed ready to pick up and go. This could be inconvenient and expensive, however, and the next best thing is to organize your painting case so that it will take all your paints and small equipment, leaving only the painting surfaces and folding easel to be carried separately. It is fatal to distribute dipper (cup), palette, knife, bottles of turps, oil etc. in other bags or in your pockets. Something will almost certainly be left behind, and anyhow it is much more difficult to get down to the actual business of painting if each piece of equipment has to be searched for.

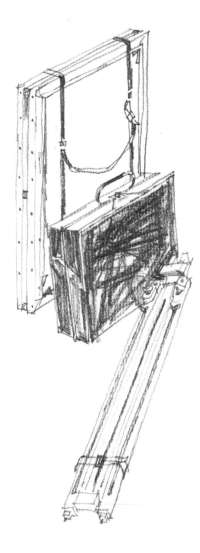

The absolute essentials for your outdoor painting case are as follows:

(i) Minimum range of tubes of colour as specified in chapter 2.

(ii) At least three brushes of the type you like - two of these should be large. One large and one small is not really enough, because you probably won't have enough turps or a big enough container to keep washing the same brush, and your picture will end up in various shades of mud.

(iii) A dipper and as large a bottle of turps as can be managed - for the above reasons.

(iv) One or two large pieces of rag, and an old newspaper.

(v) A palette as large as the box will allow.

(vi) A palette knife. If all these things will not go into one box, adapt a small suitcase or even a holdall or shopping bag. It is essential to keep everything together.

Next, the canvases or boards. The only really practical way to carry a painting so that it is not damaged while wet, is to put it face to face with a second painting surface, separating the two with canvas pins. (These pins are available at most art materials shops.) Four are sufficient to hold surfaces up to, say, 20" x 16": six will be better for larger sizes.

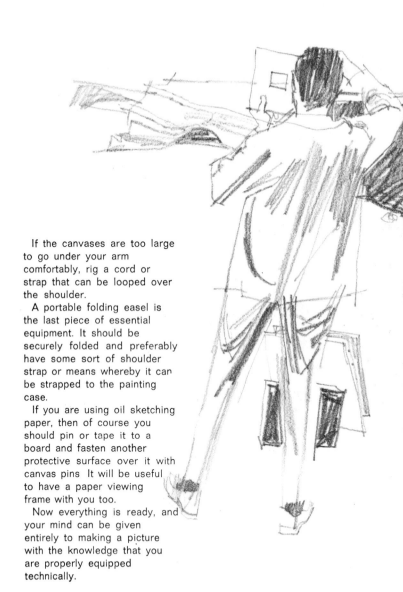

If the canvases are too large to go under your arm comfortably, rig a cord or strap that can be looped over the shoulder.

A portable folding easel is the last piece of essential equipment. It should be securely folded and preferably have some sort of shoulder strap or means whereby it can be strapped to the painting case.

If you are using oil sketching paper, then of course you should pin or tape it to a board and fasten another protective surface over it with canvas pins It will be useful to have a paper viewing frame with you too.

Now everything is ready, and your mind can be given entirely to making a picture with the knowledge that you are properly equipped technically.

I think it best to devote a whole day to painting outdoors, not because it is always necessary to take all day over a painting, but because as often as not the first drawing is tight and tentative, and it is good to have time to start afresh. So, if you can, get up early (near dawn if you can bear it), and go to an area of countryside that you like or have previously noted as worth painting.

On your way keep your eyes open and be receptive to the landscape about you. You should always do this anyway, and not just when out for a day's painting, for you must be good at looking before you can be good at painting. When you see something that interests you, don't spend too much time searching for views that might be even better. There might be other views that are better, in fact there are almost certain to be, but if you spend all day looking for them you will come back with no painting done. I don't mean that you should just start painting anywhere without thought; but if the sight of a particular piece of landscape stops you, then it is worth sitting down and trying to find out and express what it was that impressed you. I have said you must look, but you must also paint. There is no substitute for actually handling and applying paint. I firmly believe that too much thinking about it and waiting for inspiration ends in frustration and disappointment. So if you find yourself wandering from place to place in an agony of indecision, just stop anywhere and draw what is in front of you - make something out of it whatever it is.

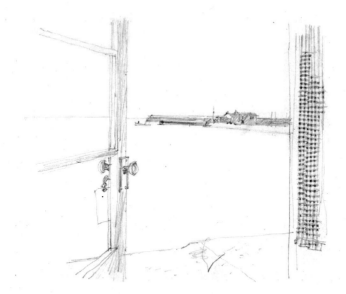

In the sketch opposite, I have done just that. I was sitting by the harbour at Lyme Regis, writing this book, and to demonstrate the principle I drew exactly what I saw in front of me, without changing my position, without in anyway modifying the view, or being very selective, or consciously composing the picture. I just drew what I saw when I looked up from my pad, and as you can see, it's quite a reasonable composition. It is very unlikely that I would have chosen this position to draw from, but having forced myself to draw what was in front of me, I found a composition which would otherwise have been passed over.

It doesn't always work, of course. Above is a drawing done from a beach hut on the sea front in which I sometimes work. It is only a few hundred yards from the spot from which the previous composition was drawn. I don't say it would be impossible to produce a painting from the very stark and simple composition which resulted, but it would be rather difficult. A view seen through a window is not strictly in its proper place in a chapter on painting out-of-doors, but it is landscape painting and can be fascinating, especially if you let the actual window frame and perhaps

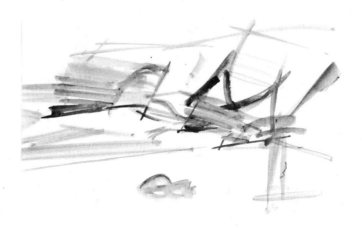

the coloured curtaining or a balcony become part of the composition. Many painters have made use of this; Pierre Bonnard, for instance, and Henri Mattise have made splendid use of the frame within a frame when looking out at landscapes through a window.

Anyway, let us assume that you have decided on a subject, prepared your equipment and are ready to paint. Spend a little time looking for the big shapes and deciding how to place them on your board, just as you did with the still life. I don't suppose you will see all the patterns that are there straightaway - they will become more obvious as you paint. But the main shapes will probably be apparent, and it is these that must be put down first. Remember, no matter how realistic you want your painting to look eventually, if it is going to be anything more than a dull piece of photographic reportage, you must put your first shapes down in such a way that they divide up the white oblong of your board in an interesting, abstract way. Proceed as before: apply thin paint at first, so that your picture dries quickly and can be modified easily; then, as the main tones and

shapes begin to look right, you can introduce fatter paint. In a one day painting there is no time for much over-painting, so once you begin to use thicker paint it is extremely important to apply the exact colour first time. Painting into sticky colour will get you into a mess, and the only way out then is to scrape down and start afresh.

Pp. 73-4 show stages in a one day outdoor sketch of the cliff and beach at Kilve in north Somerset.

It is part of a very desolate and dramatic coastline where the old fossil-bearing rock strata are clearly defined, making fantastic patterns. These strata are in evidence on the beach as well as in the cliff-face, giving an unusually powerful impression of the structural skeleton of the normally more amply covered earth. The rock has been crushed and twisted by enormous pressures over millions of years, and it is the patterns so formed which we have to sort out and draw. I have tried to subordinate other things such as light and colour, to emphasize this. Such patterns, resulting from natural forces, are everywhere, and they always have their own impeccable logic. Do not be fooled by the apparently

haphazard shapes of trees and other growing things; each
has its own characteristic structure. Every branch helps to
balance the tree, and the whole structure stands firm
against the prevailing wind, combining with its neighbours
to make the least resistant shape. So look carefully for the
precise shape and form of groups of trees and vegetation-
nebulous balls of green cotton wool just will not do.

I have emphasized the necessity of seeing and rendering
things in simple broad terms, but this does not mean that
one should never be prepared to work painstakingly on
small, fiddling detail. Sometimes a passage of carefully
rendered small pattern is just what is needed to balance a
large space - the harbour wall on p. 78 is an example.

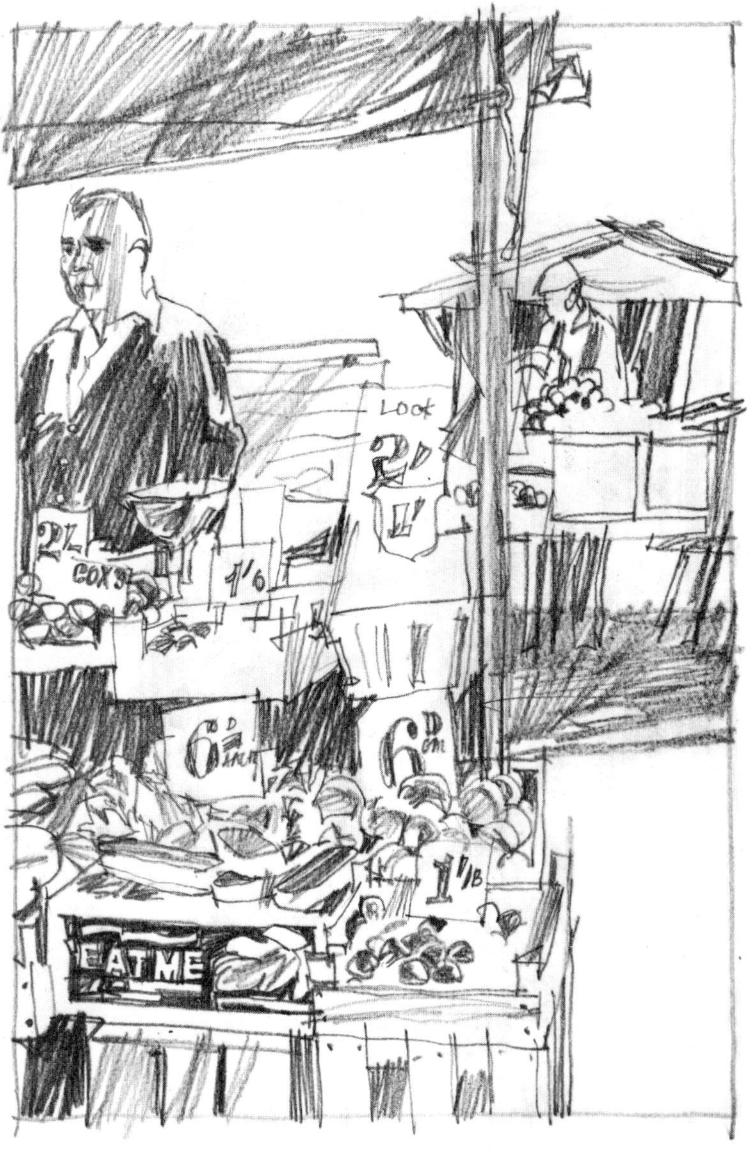
LOOK
COX'S
1'6
EAT ME

Line and wash sketch of beech trees

Lastly, I would like to mention easels again. I have not yet found an outdoor easel which does its job really efficiently. Either it is too flimsy to hold the canvas steady or even to stand up in any sort of breeze, or else it is much too heavy and cumbersome to carry. You may be luckier, but if you encounter the same difficulty, I suggest that you consider dispensing with an easel altogether. Instead, take a fairly thick board of plywood or similar material, and a small, light sketching stool. If the board is fixed to the back of your painting surface, so as to give some weight to it, you will nearly always be able to find or fabricate something round about to prop it against. It is even possible to work, as I have done on occasions, sitting on the ground, propping the canvas between my knees. It is not overcomfortable for very long, but less nerve-racking than chasing a wet airborne canvas every five minutes!

10 Photography

The artist need not be ashamed of familiarity with, and discriminating use of, the camera. Many painters have felt suspicion and mistrust of the twentieth-century photographic revolution, but I think this is a faint-hearted, head-in-the-sand attitude. Properly used, the camera is just another

extremely useful implement to supplement and assist one's own eye and hand. I am quite sure that Michelangelo would have used photography if it had been available, and Leonardo da Vinci tried his best to invent it.

In a very small space I will try to tell you enough about camera operation to ensure reliably informative photographs. The information so gained will be additional to your own drawing and observation, and should not replace it.

The camera is basically a device for exposing a light-sensitive film to an image. The image of an external object is focussed on the film by a lens, and most cameras have a means of adjusting the focus of the lens according to the distance of the subject.

The amount of light reaching the film is normally controlled in two ways. Firstly, the hole through which light enters the camera can be made larger or smaller. This is normally called the aperture of the camera, and there is an internationally accepted system for referring to aperture sizes. The largest aperture paradoxically has the smallest number, and the sizes are so arranged that going up the numerical scale each succeeding aperture admits exactly half the amount of light of the one before. Thus f/2.8 admits twice as much light as f/4, which in turn is twice as large as f/5.6, and so on.

The other way of controlling the amount of light received by the film is by the duration of the exposure. For this, a shutter is used, and it is arranged, like the aperture, so that each shutter speed gives double the exposure of the next one down (or half the next one up). The diagrams on p. 82 make this clear I hope, and it should be noted that each horizontal combination of shutter and aperture gives the same exposure to the film, since, going down the page, each succeeding aperture halves the exposure while each speed doubles it. This means that in any given light situation most cameras will offer at least six different combinations of aperture and shutter speed, all of which will expose the film correctly.

The seven pairs on p. 82 would be the correct exposures for a medium speed film on a cloudy summer day. To choose which of the available combinations of speed and aperture to use, you must first decide what sort of photograph you want. On p. 83, all the photographs were taken in the same light and from a similar position.

Pictures 1 and 2 are enlargements of the rose on which the camera was focussed at three feet, and these two very different results were obtained entirely by the use of different combinations of shutter speed and aperture. A large aperture and a high shutter speed, f/2.8 at 1/500th second, were used for the top picture. As you can see, the effect of a large aperture is to reduce the amount of the picture which is in sharp focus. The crispness of the flower against the blurred background was enhanced by the high shutter speed, which froze its movement in the breeze.

For photograph 2, the aperture was reduced in size to f/16, with the result that the background is in much sharper focus even though the distance scale on the camera was still set to focus at three feet on the flower. The slow shutter speed of 1/15th second, which had to be used with f/16, has allowed subject movement and camera shake to soften the whole image somewhat, indeed a camera really should be on a tripod at any speed slower than 1/30th second. If the background is to be the main interest, the focus must be changed as in photograph 3. Here my daughter entered the picture, and so without changing the camera position, I adjusted the focus to 15 feet.

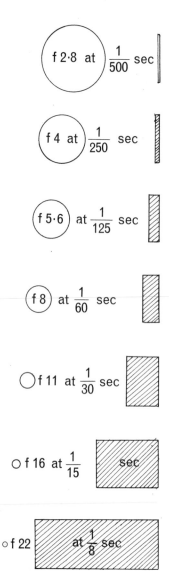

A shutter speed of 1/60th second was sufficiently fast to stop the relatively slow movement of the figure, and the aperture of f/8 rendered middle ground and background in focus while blurring the near flower.

To achieve overall sharp focus, one must move the camera further away from the foreground object, in this case, the rose. This is the only difference in procedure between photographs 3 and 4. The exposure was left at 1/60th second at f/8 and the focus at 15 feet, but the camera was moved back to about 10 feet from the rose, thereby bringing it within the depth of focus (in this case from about 10 feet to 35 feet), and as you can see everything is fairly sharp.

I repeat, the exposure and focus you choose depends on what sort of picture you want. Selective focus, subject movement and even severe camera movement can produce very interesting photographs, frequently strongly evocative of paintings, so don't necessarily throw away those blurred prints!

Finally, I have included a chart giving a rough guide to the sort of exposures necessary in different light conditions. I have assumed for this purpose that it is spring or summertime and that black and white film of medium speed (i.e. about 125 to 150 ASA) is being used. If film such as 50 ASA colour film, which is only half this speed, is used, then all exposures would have to be doubled (one aperture larger or one shutter speed slower) and so on. Also in winter, except in sunlit snow conditions, the exposure will probably need to be doubled. A light meter is ideal, of course, especially for colour film, which needs a more exact exposure, but for most purposes you will find this rough guide will not be far out.

Remember that it is information that we are after: information to help amplify or complete a painting begun from direct observation. Imitation of the photograph itself is pointless and boring.

Film speed: 125 A.S.A.

Conditions / Speed	Light interior away from window	Light interior by window	Outdoors cloudy dull	Outdoors cloudy bright	Outdoors bright sun	Outdoors very bright snow, beach
$\frac{1}{250}$	1	2	4	5·6	8	11
$\frac{1}{125}$	1·4	2·8	5·6	8	11	16
$\frac{1}{60}$	2	4	8	11	16	22
$\frac{1}{30}$	2·8	5·6	11	16	22	32
$\frac{1}{15}$	4	8	16	22	32	64

Shaded squares are not commenly available apertures.

11 Pattern making

By putting this chapter near the end of the book, after the objective painting chapters, I do not mean to suggest some intrinsic change which could merit a clearcut decision to 'go abstract'.

All paintings are abstract in the sense that they are two dimensional arrangements of shape, colour, line, tone etc. which symbolize, represent or suggest things or ideas. The extent to which any original observation or experience is recognized in a painting, is a measure of the acceptability of the language of symbolism used. Paintings can be highly naturalistic, i.e., very close to what most people see or what the camera sees, or they can be highly organized and simplified into shapes which are not so immediately obvious and recognizable. But either way, the painting will only be good if the design is good.

So let us not be too worried if careful observation and analysis of the objective world leads us to patterns of shape and colour which begin to have a reality of their own and do not rely on slavish imitation of surface appearances.

Our normal everyday view of the world is extremely limited: only one side of the exterior of objects of a certain size

Abstract painting: based on electronic circuitry

is normally perceived at any one time. Because most things seen in this way are familiar and meaningful in other ways, we tend not to notice their visual pattern. Change the scale though, by looking through a microscope or going up in an aircraft, and suddenly we seem to be seeing abstract pictures.

The illustration at the head of this chapter is a photograph. The tonal contrast has been increased but basically it remains a literal view of an actual object. It is, in fact, a photograph of crystals formed in the bottom of a photographic dish. Lack of context and recognition makes it abstract. Natural abstract patterns, incidentally, are frequently more exciting than any that one tries to conceive from imagination. In any case, it is debatable whether one's imagination does not consist entirely of images seen at one time or another and unconsciously registered.

The point of all this, I suggest, is that it is unnecessary to make strong distinctions between representational and abstract paintings. The difference between paintings which consist of absolutely flat patterns and those which use the illusion of depth and space, is to my mind much more considerable. I personally prefer painting to be of the latter kind: there seems to be so much more scope for interplay of surfaces and colours once the possibility of recession and space is accepted.

Look for the planes and the patterns, put them down simply and with conviction, and don't worry too much about the people who ask what it is, or which way up it is.

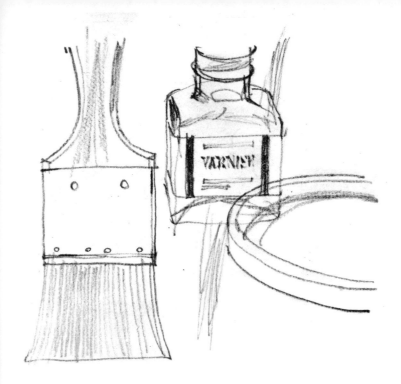

12 Varnishing and framing

Completed oil paintings are varnished for two reasons. Firstly, to bring up any colour that has gone flat and thereby make the picture equally visible in all parts, and secondly, to protect it from the harmful effects of the atmosphere and moisture.

It is imperative that the picture should be absolutely dry before attempting to apply varnish. Thorough drying and hardening can take months or even a year, and it is usually considered necessary to wait at least a year before it is safe to varnish an oil painting. Premature varnishing will cause cracking of the layers of colour.

As for the type of varnish to use, while mastic and dammar ethereal varnishes are normally acceptable, they are sometimes adversely affected by certain paints and mediums which they may have to cover, such as megilp (pale drying oil of linseed and double mastic varnish). Most manufacturers now produce very reliable synthetic resin in white spirit varnishes. These do not yellow or bloom, and always remain slightly flexible and therefore resistant to cracking. They are not so glass-hard as the older varnishes, but they are easily removed and can therefore be renewed from time to time.

Suppose then that the painting *has* completely dried; the varnish should be applied in a dust free room on a warm dry day with a warm brush. Even the painting should be warmed (both sides), so as to get rid of any condensation which would cause the varnish to bloom and go cloudy. If the picture has become just a little grubby, bread or kneaded rubber can be used to clean it: but if it has become really dirty, it may be necessary to wash it gently with soap and water, after which of course it must be thoroughly dried. Apply the varnish from a shallow dish with a large flat brush. It is sometimes easier to treat heavily painted areas (impasto) with a cloth dipped in varnish and pressed lightly on the picture. Allow to dry in an even temperature and a dust free atmosphere.

Framing a picture, especially a large oil painting, can be very expensive. It is very much cheaper if you make the frames yourself, and it is not all that difficult. Special picture mouldings can be bought in lengths to be cut and mitred, but they are fairly expensive, frequently over-ornate and if large are difficult to mitre without special equipment. On the other hand, there are many standard mouldings in general use for building purposes which can be purchased comparatively cheaply. They can be cut and mitred separately and combined in a great variety of ways to make interesting composite mouldings such as those suggested on p. 93.

Absolutely essential for frame making is a mitreblock, which is a device for directing a 45° saw cut through the firmly held moulding. The best ones are made of metal, but a wooden one will do. Make sure that it has cutting guides at least 3 inches high, preferably more. This will enable you to mitre wood held on its edge.

Almost as essential as the mitre-block is at least one corner cramp. This is a sort of right-angled vice for holding two mitred edges together while they are glued and pinned

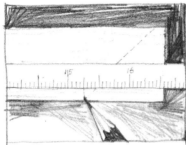

First mitre one end of a length of the flat timber. Then place it against one side of the canvas and mark the inside length so that it is a little longer than the canvas.

Cut the mitre from the mark to the longer outside edge. Use this piece to measure and cut another identical to it. Repeat for the two shorter sides.

Mitre one end of the chamfered architrave and the scotia mouldings. Place them with one of the flat pieces so that the mitres at one end line up and mark them off against the mitre at the other end. Repeat for the other three sides.

Apply strong glue to the two mitres to be joined and bring them firmly together in the corner cramp. Pin with panel pins (brads) as shown overleaf. Repeat for all four corners. Glue and pin outer and inner mouldings as shown.

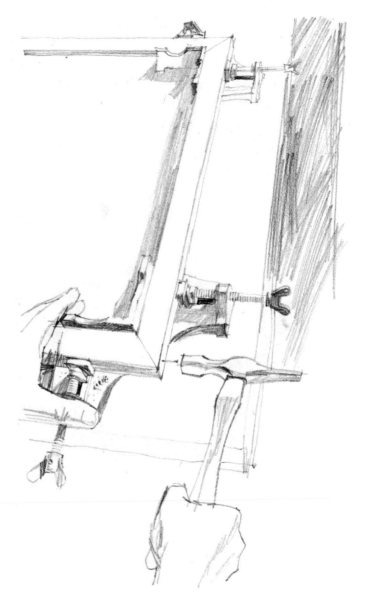

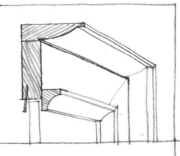

1″ x 3″ planed timber, 2½″ x 3¾″ chamfered architrave and 1″ x ¾″ scotia. The flat face could be covered with canvas or coloured.

4″ x ½″ planed timber, 4″ x 1″ planed timber, 1″ x ⅜″ parting bead. The flat surface and/or the edge can be coloured subtly.

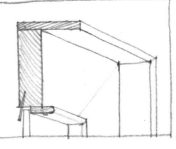

2½″ x ¾″ chamfered architrave, 1″ x ¾″ scotia, and half a dozen or so blocks of wood to locate canvas. Better painted all white - perhaps a little colour on outer edge only.

2″ moulded architrave and 1″ x ¾″ scotia. The frames shown above and right are better for smaller paintings.

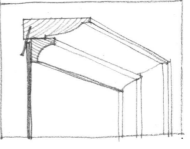

(see p. 92). A tenon saw, long and deep enough for the mitre-block, a hammer, rule, panel pins (brads) and glue are the remaining necessities. Diagrams and notes on p. 93 describe the procedure, which is quite straightforward and simple, provided that the mitres are cut carefully and accurately.

Some paintings look well with nothing but a thin, plain batten of wood around them or even a metal edging. It all depends on the picture and its possible location, and personal preference must be your guide. Having finished the frame, it can be painted flat white and colour applied sparingly to parts of it if needed. Flat faces of the frame can be covered with canvas or hessian (burlap) glued on, and thin forward facing edges sometimes look well painted a strong colour or covered with gold leaf. I am sure that you will have many other ideas, but be careful that they do not become too obtrusive. The frame must not compete with the picture!

Oil paintings do not normally have glass in front of them, as it makes them rather difficult to see. In any case, the varnish protects them well enough without.

13 Conclusion

My intention has been to give a basic outline of the technique of oil painting and to suggest some ways of perceiving the visual world. I have purposely avoided saying much about the form that your painting should take when finished - this is something that you must decide for yourself. It probably need not even involve a conscious decision - just paint as you want to. Lack of professional competence should not deter you, in fact the most valuable asset you have as a beginner is, or should be, a fresh, open, untrained vision. The sense of wonder and delight in seeing that children have, which results in such charming unselfconscious paintings, is so often lost when adult, and is submerged even further by professional training. Many painters only rediscover this sense of wonder at the end of years and years of academic training.

It is probable that you are not as direct and uncluttered as a child: you may have acquired ideas about painting almost unconsciously from bad sources. It would be impossible to enumerate in detail the bad and good influences. All I can suggest is that you look at paintings by the acknowledged masters of past and present whenever you have the opportunity.

Try to forget anything else you have ever learnt about painting and start afresh. Paint what you like, as you like, and remember that your boredom or your enjoyment will be obvious in your painting - so enjoy yourself.

Index